WHAT AM I?

Jumpy, Green, and Croaky

WHAT AM I?

By Moira Butterfield
Illustrated by Wayne Ford

RSVP

RAINTREE
STECK-VAUGHN
PUBLISHERS
The Steck-Vaughn Company

Austin, Texas

Published by Raintree Steck-Vaughn Publishers, an imprint of Steck-Vaughn Company.

Editors: Stephanie Bellwood, Heather Luff
Project Manager: Joyce Spicer
Designer: Helen James
Illustrator: Wayne Ford / Wildlife Art Agency
Consultant: Andrew Branson

Library of Congress Cataloging-in-Publication Data

Butterfield, Moira, 1961-
    Jumpy, Green, and Croaky/by Moira Butterfield; illustrated by Wayne Ford.
        p.   cm. — (What am I?)
    Summary: A riddle asking the reader to guess which animal is being described precedes information about different parts of a frog's body, how it behaves, and where it lives.
        ISBN 0-8172-4591-X (hardcover)
        ISBN 0-8172-7226-7 (softcover)
        1. Bullfrog — Juvenile literature.   [1. Frogs.]
    I. Ford, Wayne, ill.   II. Title.   III. Series.
    QL668.E27B88   1998
    597.8'9 — dc21   96-8049
                                                 CIP   AC

Printed in Hong Kong
Bound in the United States.
1 2 3 4 5 6 7 8 9 0 WO 01 00 99 98 97

My skin is wet.
My legs are strong.
They help me jump and swim
along.
To catch a meal, I leap up high
and wrap my tongue around a fly.

What am I?

Here is my eye.

I hide in the weeds
of the pond where
I live. Only my
eyes stick up
above the water.

Can you see
my ears? They
are the big circles
behind my eyes.

Here are my back legs.

When an insect
flies over my head,
I push on my strong
back legs and leap
out of the water.

I move so fast
through the air
that this tasty moth
will not see me
coming.

Here is my tongue.

It shoots out of my mouth and wraps around the moth. Then my tongue disappears back into my mouth.

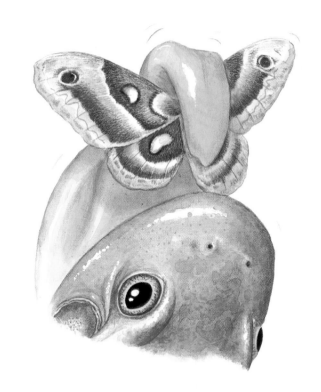

I live with all kinds of small animals like these ducklings. They like to eat the same things I do.

Here are my back feet.

They are webbed.
This means that I have
skin stretched between
each toe. It helps me
to swim fast.

My feet help me
to jump. I look out
for big animals who
want to eat me, like
that hungry heron.

13

Here are my front legs.

I have four long,
thin toes on my front
legs. I use them to
push food into
my wide mouth.

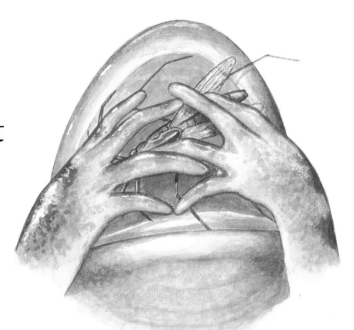

I like to sit and rest on
my front legs. I hide
in the long grass and
look for food.

15

Here is my skin.

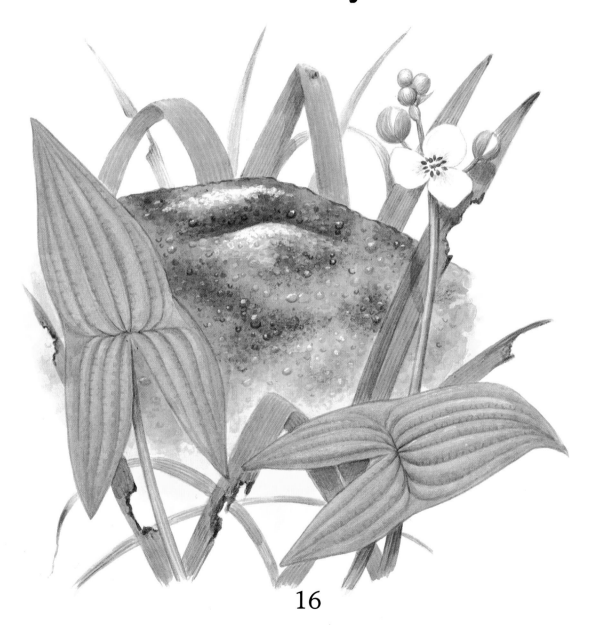

My skin is smooth
and very slippery.
It is green, gray,
and yellow. I can
hide in the green
pondweed.

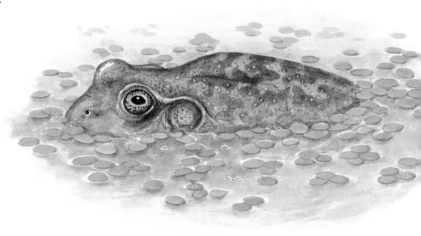

When I am underwater,
I breathe through my skin.
When I am on land,
I breathe through
my nose, like you.

17

Here is my throat.

Sometimes I call to other animals like me. I puff out my throat like a balloon and make a deep groaning noise.

You can hear me from far away ...
croak!
Have you guessed what I am?

I am a frog.

Point to my...

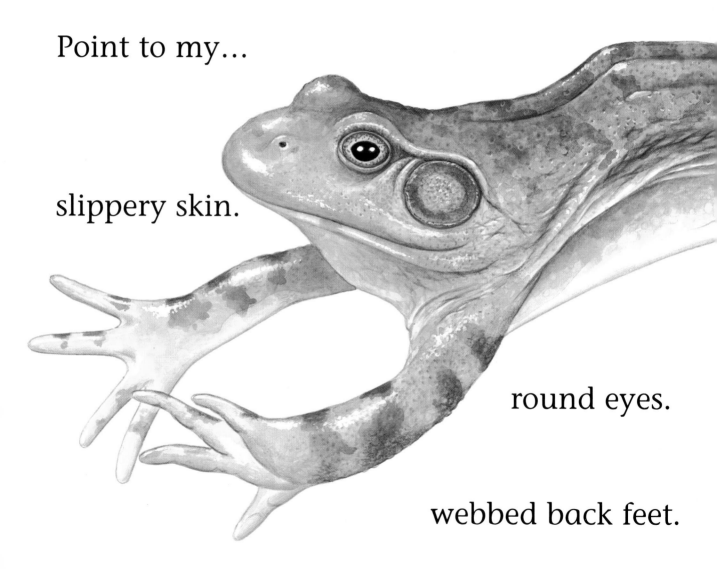

slippery skin.

round eyes.

webbed back feet.

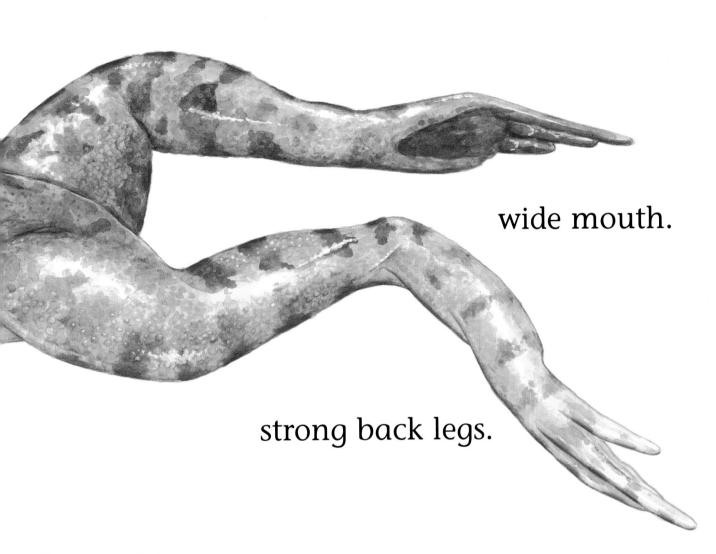

wide mouth.

strong back legs.

long, thin toes.

I am called an
American bullfrog.

21

Here is a baby bullfrog.

It starts as a tiny egg
in a lump of eggs
called frog spawn.
A tadpole hatches
out of each egg.

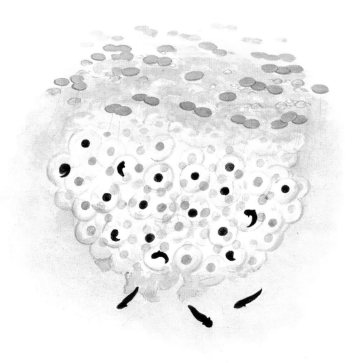

The tadpole looks
like a little fish.
Then it starts to
grow legs. Slowly
it turns into a frog.

23

Here is my home.

I live in ponds, lakes, and swamps.

How many bullfrogs can you find?
Can you see two spotted turtles,
a pond skater, and a water snake?

Here is a map of the world.

I live in
North America.
Where is it
on the map?

North
America

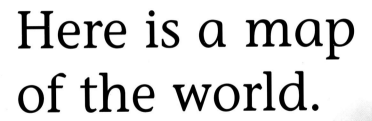

Can you point to the
place where you live?

27

Can you answer these questions about me?

What does my skin feel like?

Why are my webbed
back feet useful?

What do I like to eat?

What are baby
frogs called?

What do my
ears look like?

How do I catch
my food?

What do I use
my front legs for?

Where do I live?

What color is my skin?

Here are words to help you learn about me.

breathe To take air in and let it out of my body. This keeps me alive. I can breathe through my nose or my skin.

frog spawn A lump of frog's eggs floating in water. The eggs turn into tadpoles.

leap To make a long, high jump.

slippery Something that feels wet and is hard to hold.

tadpole The name for a baby frog. A tadpole slowly grows into a frog.

throat The back of my mouth. I blow out my throat and make a loud noise.

swamp A wet, muddy place.

webbed A webbed foot has skin stretched between each toe. My back feet are webbed.

weeds Wild plants that grow fast. Pondweed is a type of weed.